Original title:
Tides of Life's Journey

Copyright © 2025 Creative Arts Management OÜ
All rights reserved.

Author: Aurora Sinclair
ISBN HARDBACK: 978-1-80587-328-0
ISBN PAPERBACK: 978-1-80587-798-1

Whispers of the Deep

Bubbles dance like party guests,
Seaweed sways in funny vests.
Fish gossip with a flip and splash,
While crabs race by, in a hurry to dash.

A mermaid's laugh, a whale's loud cheer,
Seashells gossip, lend an ear!
Jellyfish bounce like they own the floor,
Underwater shenanigans, who could ask for more?

The Voyage of Resilience

Anchored dreams set sail with glee,
A pirate cat navigates the sea.
With a parrot that squawks out a joke,
They sail through waves on a rhythm and poke.

Storm clouds gather, but there's no dread,
As merfolk dance on the waves instead.
Every mishap met with a hearty laugh,
Turns squalls into a glorious craft.

Storms and Serenities

Raindrops tap dance on my hat,
While dolphins flip, showing off like that.
Thunder grumbles; I sip my tea,
A squall's just nature's comedy spree!

The sun peeks out, a golden wink,
The ocean's laughter makes me think.
Clouds scatter like confetti fast,
The storm's forgotten, we're back to the blast.

Footprints on Sandy Paths

Sandy toes and a squeaky laugh,
Building castles, the ultimate craft.
But watch out for the waves that sneak,
They tickle ankles, and it's all bleak!

Seagulls squawk like they run the show,
Crabs do the cha-cha, don't you know?
Each footprint tells stories, big and small,
Life takes a stroll—oh, the fun of it all!

Waves of Giggles

The ocean's laugh, a rolling spree,
With seagulls dancing, wild and free.
A crab may pinch, but what a sight,
As we all blubber in pure delight.

A boat on a wave did wobble and sway,
Captain shouting, "Let's sail away!"
With a splash and a plop, overboard flung,
The fish, they chuckled, and so we sung.

The currents pull us, left and right,
But we just giggle through the fright.
A seashell told me a quirky tale,
Of a fish that tried to ride a whale.

So here we float, with laughter strong,
Each splash and giggle, we can't go wrong.
Life's a beach, in the sun's warm glow,
Let's ride these waves, just let it flow!

Sunsets on the Journey's Path

Sunset paints the sky with glee,
As we stumble and spill our tea.
Chasing shadows, we trip and fall,
Laughter echoes, that's our call.

Sipping joy from funny cups,
While the world keeps spinning up.
With each giggle, we wave goodbye,
To mishaps that make us fly high.

Ripples of Remembered Moments

Each splash a tale of what went wrong,
A fish that danced, a seaweed song.
Remember that time we lost the map?
We ended up napping in the lap.

Rippling laughter fills the air,
When we find a crab with green hair.
Moments like this, we'll always share,
In the ocean's humor, we're a pair.

The Sea of Our Changing Seasons

Winter's chill brings snowballs of fun,
Missed that shot? Let's run! Let's run!
Summer's sun makes us sweat and melt,
With popsicle sticks, our troubles dealt.

Autumn leaves swirl, a dance so fine,
We twirl around with pumpkin wine.
Spring brings blooms that we can't ignore,
But sneezing from pollen? We ask for more!

Navigating the Waters of Tomorrow

With a compass that points to 'fun',
We sail on waves, our laughter spun.
Each wave a glitch, a giggle found,
Our ship's a laughingstock, all around.

Tomorrow's forecast? High on cheer,
Winds of fortune, steering near.
We'll chart the course with silly mistakes,
As we dance on deck, the ocean quakes.

Reflections in the Surging Sea

Waves crashing with a cheeky grin,
Saltwater tickles, let the fun begin.
Seagulls squawk, they've got jokes to tell,
As I slip on my flip-flops, oh well!

Beachball battles, who's lost the game?
Sand in my sandwich? Oh, what a shame!
But laughter echoes through the salty air,
Life's a splash, let's dance without a care.

Embracing the Flow

The river chuckles as it swirls around,
Splashing my shoes; look, I'm a drowned clown!
A floaty kayak, or a brave cannonball?
Either way, I'm bound to have a ball.

Water fights ignite with silly squeals,
Splashing like dolphins, it's all about feels.
Waves of laughter, we sail through the bliss,
Floating on joy, who could ask for more than this?

The Ebb and Flow of Time

Time slips away like an ice cream cone,
Melting in sunshine, yeah, we've all known.
The clock ticks backward, or does that seem right?
I swear I was five just last Saturday night.

Moments rush by like a runaway train,
Picking up speed just to drive us insane.
But who can blame time? It loves a good jest,
In the comedy of life, we're all just a guest.

Navigating Uncharted Waters

Maps are for sailors, I'm lost in the blue,
Waves guide my heart, can you trust the view?
I'm paddling hard with a grin and a laugh,
Hoping this boat won't end up in half!

Charts drawn in crayons, oh what a sight,
Adventure awaits, let's set sail tonight.
Mermaids may giggle as we splash down the lane,
With a wink and a nudge, they'll drive us insane!

The Art of Sinking

In a boat made of dreams, I row,
With oars that are paddles of dough.
Every dip and each splash, I find,
Naps come easy, I'm one of a kind.

Fish laugh as they swim away,
"Is that guy trying to make a bouquet?"
With every puff of air I exhale,
I wonder if my ship is for sale.

Cycles of the Sea

Waves crash like jokes on the shore,
Knocking sand castles down, what a chore!
I build up high, but they tumble low,
Maybe my bucket's designed to overflow?

Mermaids giggle at my sand woes,
While chasing their tails, where nobody goes.
Swimmers treat the pool like a stage,
Flipping their flops in a salty rage.

Remnants of Forgotten Shores

Old flip-flops found on the beach,
A message in a bottle's in reach.
The crabs read my diary, oh dear,
They laugh at my dating life—what a leer!

Seagulls squawk, thinking it's news,
As I muse over my surfboard blues.
Each grain of sand tells tales so great,
Of sunburns and burgers on my plate.

A Sea of Possibilities

A cup of coffee spills on the deck,
Distractions abound—what the heck!
I see a dolphin, pulling a prank,
While sharks nibble at my tin can tank.

With each splash, the sun shines bright,
We dance on waves, oh what a sight!
Life's an ocean, full of fun,
Just don't forget your friend, the sun!

Embracing the Unknown

With every turn, I lose my mind,
Trying to find what's left behind.
A map that leads to hidden cheese,
Or just a sock with holes and fleas.

Adventures beckon, oh what fun,
Like chasing cats that never run.
I stumble forth, I trip and fall,
But that's just part of the great sprawl.

The Drift of Dreams

In sleep I sail on boats of cheese,
With a crew of squirrels—if you please!
They sing of nuts and acorn charms,
While I just nap in fluffy arms.

I drift along on fluffy clouds,
Wearing pajamas, feeling proud.
Yet morning calls, and dreams take flight,
As I wake up with bedhead fright.

Waters of Reflection

I peer into the pond so clear,
And see a frog staring back near.
He croaks, 'You've got some funny hair!'
I laugh and splash without a care.

Ripples dance like a wiggly worm,
Reflecting me in every term.
'This water's deep,' the wise frog quips,
'But you're just sinking, check those flips!'

Searching for Safe Harbor

I searched for solace on a shore,
Where seagulls squawk and people snore.
With cooler full of snacks galore,
Is safety found? I'm not so sure.

Someone shouted, 'Grab that wave!'
I'm in a boat—no, I'm a knave!
Capped with ice cream, dark and sweet,
I paddle hard—my legs feel beat!

Beneath a Starlit Sky

Under a sky with twinkling teens,
We dance like ants in our silly dreams.
Stars winking down, like they know the jest,
While we trip on shoes that are far from best.

Laughter echoes, a symphony in flight,
As we wrestle shadows in the pale moonlight.
A comet zips past, it's quite the show,
But my drink just spilled, oh well, here we go!

Circles of Belonging

Around the fire, we roast some fries,
With laughter that dances, like fireflies.
Each friend's a puzzle piece, just a bit odd,
Fitting together, how strange we applaud!

We jive in circles, with snacks and tea,
Who knew that weirdness felt so carefree?
We share our quirks, a wild parade,
As we all agree, normal's overrated!

The Language of Water

Water whispers secrets, gurgles and splashes,
It tells fish tales of epic high clashes.
A droplet hops, then slips, oh dear!
"Water you doing?" shouts another near!

Waves crash like jokes that just never land,
While rivers chuckle, oh isn't it grand?
Sprinklers spray laughter, a fresh comedy,
In every puddle, life's a bit silly!

An Anchor in Time

Time's a shipwreck, we sail with glee,
Finding treasure in each memory.
With anchors of laughter to hold us tight,
In storms of stress, we dance through the night.

Moments like bubbles, they burst and float,
We paddle with purpose, on this strange boat.
Yet here we are, with winds so bizarre,
Still laughing all the way, oh what a star!

Sailboats on the Infinite Blue

On a sailboat that's oh-so-small,
I thought I'd conquer waves and all.
Yet there I sat, a chicken tied,
With fishy friends who joined the ride.

We waved to folks on sunny shores,
While ducks shot past, all quack and roars.
I raised my sails with hopeful cheer,
But winds just whispered, 'Not this year!'

The Rhythm of Surging Days

Life's a dance with silly shoes,
Sometimes we win, sometimes we lose.
I trip and tumble with a grin,
For every fall, there's joy within.

My calendar's a jumbled mess,
With meetings lost and chance to rest.
Yet every bump and goofy twist,
Reminds me that I can't resist!

Footprints in the Shifting Sand

On the beach, footprints are made,
I stumble, slip, and somehow trade.
For every step that I might take,
The beach just laughs at my mistake.

Waves come crashing, sweeping fast,
My grand designs are gone at last.
Yet as I giggle at the chase,
The ocean leaves a soggy trace.

Skylines and Sailors

Sailors gaze at the crowded sky,
While seagulls take their food supply.
We aim for laughter, cast our nets,
But end up tangled in our debts.

With skyline views and smoothies bright,
We toast our glasses, what a sight!
For every sailor's tale that's spun,
There's always fun when day is done.

Currents of Compassion

In the ocean's vast embrace,
We paddle with a smiley face,
Sometimes we drift, sometimes we glide,
With rubber ducks as our guide!

A seagull swoops, with a cheeky grin,
Dives for chips, oh where to begin?
With laughter echoing in the breeze,
Life's a ride, so snack with ease!

We wave at strangers, what a sight,
Frogs and fish join in the night,
With every splash, a giggle grows,
Unexpected friends, who could've known?

Through each twist, through every turn,
Compassion's lesson, oh how we learn,
As jellyfish dance and crabs run wild,
It's a quirky trip, so run, sea child!

Navigating Through Shadows

With a map that's filled with scribbles,
We sail where seaweed giggles,
Avoiding waves that look like frowns,
In this sea of ups and downs!

The sun dips low, we're lost, it's true,
But then a whale joins in the brew,
With songs of sass and jokes to tell,
Floating on, we're under their spell!

Dark clouds creep, oh what a bind,
But humor's the anchor we will find,
For even storms can't steal the fun,
We surf the chaos, everyone!

So we'll wave at gloom and dance with fog,
Trading tales like an old sea dog,
Navigating shadows with a cheer,
Our laughter echoes loud and clear!

Seabeds of Memory

The sands of time, oh how they shift,
In each grain lies a silly gift,
Buried treasure and dancing crabs,
Memories made in jest, no drabs!

Old boats float like dreams that snore,
Each ripple whispers 'come explore',
We dig for gold, find only shells,
But giggles abound in our tales and yells!

Seashell friends come out to play,
With laughter scattered on the bay,
Fish tell stories of life's great chase,
While starfish wink with a goofy face!

So let's splash in the shallow seas,
Collecting memories with playful ease,
In this vibrant world of winks and cheers,
We'll treasure the laughter through all our years!

Journey Through the Foam

Foamy waves, oh what a blast,
They tickle toes as we sail past,
Jumping high, we splash and squeal,
In this wacky dream, it's all surreal!

With a beach ball bouncing through the air,
Seagulls peek with curious flair,
We play tag with the frothy crest,
In this salty dance, we laugh the best!

Umbrellas twirl like spinning tops,
Sandcastles wobble, but never flop,
As crabs keep time with their own kind of beat,
We groove along, oh this is sweet!

So let the waves take us afar,
Where giggles echo like a pop star,
In a whirl of foam, both wild and free,
We embrace the joy of simply being me!

Floating Between Moments

I once lost my sock in the wash,
It giggled away, such a posh.
Waves of laundry, oh what a joke,
Swirling around like a mad folk.

The cat thinks it's a cozy bed,
As I trip over the things I said.
Floating in chaos, a dance so spry,
Guess it's fun to be a little shy.

I drift in the chaos, seeking peace,
Finding my cereal, a puzzle at least.
Sailing through breakfast, lost in a bowl,
Where's my spoon? Oh, that's rock and roll!

Life's a float on this big wacky sea,
With dishes that dance and shoes that flee.
I'll laugh with the waves as they come and go,
Floating 'til my next wacky show.

The Horizon Beckons

With a sandwich in hand, I set to sail,
But the seagulls above have a grander tale.
They swoop and they dive, a heist in the air,
Leaving me wondering, was lunch really there?

The horizon winks, a mischievous tease,
Whispers of adventure ride the cool breeze.
I chase after dreams with a haphazard stride,
And trip on my shoelaces—I take it in stride.

The sun casts a shadow that looks just like me,
Stretched out in laughter, a sight to see.
I wave to the clouds, all fluffy and bright,
They giggle back softly, just out of sight.

So here I am, on this journey of mirth,
Finding the joy in the chaos of earth.
With each silly step, I'll dance with delight,
The horizon's my buddy, let's take to flight.

Beneath the Surface

What lurks beneath in the washing machine?
A kingdom of socks, oh what a scene!
The sudsy fish swim with bubbles of loot,
Dancing around in a slippery clute.

Under the bed, my keys start to hide,
A treasure chest waiting, a wild ride.
With chairs as the ship and dust bunnies crew,
We sail past the cat—what a view!

On rainy days, I dive deep in thought,
Searching for answers that I never caught.
The puddles act as mirrors, reflecting my fate,
Should I jump in? Nah, I'll just contemplate.

Each splash tells a story of laughter and glee,
Life's underwater circus, come play with me.
We'll float on the whims of whatever may come,
This journey's a riddle—the punchline, a drum!

Ripples of Fate

In the pond of choices, I tossed a stone,
The ripples spread quickly, making me groan.
Why did I choose the blue over green?
Now fish are judging me, oh how obscene!

The neighbor's dog has a knack for surprise,
He leaps for the ball but dives for the flies.
With each woof that echoes, I can't help but laugh,
His silly antics are a glorious gaff.

Sometimes I ponder, as I wave to the sun,
Is life just a joke or a long, wild run?
Perhaps it's both, with a side of ice cream,
The laughter and sweetness make a perfect team.

So here's to the ripples, the twists, and the cheer,
I'll surf on the giggles throughout the whole year.
With a wink and a grin, I'll embrace what appears,
In the comedy show of our everyday fears.

Anchoring Dreams

A boat that dreams of being grand,
Sails with hopes, too big to stand.
Yet here it bobs, so close to shore,
And wonders what it's meant for more.

The anchor's stuck, it won't let go,
It's holding tight, just like a pro.
While seagulls laugh and steal my snacks,
I ponder if I've hit the racks.

Fish swim by in a curious lane,
They mock my hopes of being vain.
I wish to sail to lands unknown,
But here I am, in this old zone.

As dreams float by, I take a sip,
Of salty air and citrus grip.
Who needs the sea when one can dream,
Of adventures lost in some ice cream?

The Shoreline of Tomorrow

On the shore where sands do play,
I built a castle, come what may.
The tide rolled in, my prize to claim,
And all I got was such a shame.

Crabs marched in, my guards of fate,
Declaring war, could I escape?
With buckets full of dreams gone wild,
I learned that laughter's always styled.

Each wave that crashes, sets anew,
A joke of life, it comes in two.
So as I chase my fleeting prize,
I trip on shells, oh how time flies!

The future's bright, with jokes abound,
I'll find my way, and sail around.
For every grain that slips away,
I'll toss a joke, and call it play!

Unfurling Sail of Destiny

The sail unfurls, a mighty feat,
Like breakfast toast, a joy to eat.
With winds bestowed, my fate is clear,
But first, must find a place to steer.

I tug and pull, the ropes entwine,
While seagulls squawk, 'You're doing fine!'
I shout back, 'Oh, is that so?',
As I stumble on the deck below.

As waves approach, they greet me loud,
With laughter shared, I'm part of the crowd.
The ocean's punchlines toss and tease,
But I just smile, and try to please.

At last, my course is set to roam,
With dreams afloat, I'm far from home.
With every sway and silly spin,
I'm just the captain, let's begin!

Moonlit Tides

Beneath the moon, the waters gleam,
A silver light, a sailing dream.
The fish are laughing, oh what fun,
While crabs compete for who can run.

I raised a toast to stars above,
And joined their dance, it fits like glove.
Yet in my zeal to join the jest,
I tripped on waves and lost my quest.

The moonlight giggles as I glide,
With every splash, my hopes collide.
But being lost is part of the game,
Since life's a jest, and I'm to blame!

So here I float, a fool in glee,
With dreams wrapped tight in irony.
Each wave a laugh, a grin so bold,
In moonlit tides, my heart won't fold.

Drift of Time

Time floats by like a pesky bug,
It teases the clock with a silly shrug.
Minutes turn hours, then back to two,
As if the universe's playing peek-a-boo.

Got plans today? Well, three days ago,
My calendar laughed, said 'no can do, bro!'
I'll chase my dreams like a dog with a bone,
But first, where's my sock? Oh, it's time to roam.

Like jelly on toast, it's all a bit spread,
I'll dance through the chaos, keep moving ahead.
With every new laugh, the seconds warp round,
Each chuckle a wave, making life more profound.

In this merry-go-round, I find my delight,
Laughing at snafus, oh what a sight!
So cheers to the moments, both silly and grand,
For drifting through time, oh isn't it grand?

Rising with the Dawn

The sun peeks in with a cheeky grin,
Bidding the night a hilarious spin.
Birds crack jokes perched on the trees,
While I wrestle my blanket, say 'give me some peace!'

I stumble to coffee, the potion of life,
Pajamas still clinging, I'm ready for strife.
The toast pops up like a surprise from a show,
Burnt edges waving, saying 'how do you do?'

With breakfast a circus, I laugh with delight,
Juggling the dishes, oh what a sight!
Each plate a performer, in this show I call mine,
Comedy rising like my morning caffeine line.

So here's to the day, as it brightens my fate,
With giggles and grumbles, I'm ready, don't wait!
We rise with the dawn, with a wink and a nudge,
Embracing the oddness that life will not judge.

The Calm Before

There's a moment of quiet, it's oddly serene,
Like a cat with a fishbowl, or a screen with a meme.
The world holds its breath, then cracks up in glee,
Just waiting for chaos to give life a spree.

I sit with my tea, while the universe zips,
Planning my day like a juggler's flips.
Will this sock match? Will I find my keys?
The calm before madness can be such a tease.

A hiccup in time, like a giggle that pops,
A moment of silence before laughter drops.
With a wink and a grin, I brace for the show,
Life's punchlines await, as I just sit and glow.

So let's savor the stillness, the pause, the 'whoa'—
Before the craziness sweeps in like a show.
In this calm before thrill, let's sip and enjoy,
For laughter is coming, life's favorite ploy.

Shadows of the Swell

Waves rolling in with a comical twist,
They tickle my toes, oh how can I resist?
Each splash a reminder that joy's all around,
As the shadows of swell dance and abound.

Flip-flops forgotten, I'm dancing in sand,
The sea whispers jokes that I can understand.
With each rising wave, I'm swept in its humor,
Like a sitcom unfolding in this sandy rumor.

Surfers like jesters, they ride with such style,
Crashing and laughing, they go the extra mile.
The ocean's a stand-up, with punchlines galore,
Every crest and every fall ignites a thunderous roar.

So cheers to the waves, their playful embrace,
Carrying laughter in this watery space.
In the shadows they cast, let's giggle and dwell,
For life's absurd charm is the best story to tell.

Driftwood Dreams

A piece of wood on the shore,
It dreams of being much more.
'Twas once a tree, you see,
Now a raft for a squirrel's spree.

It floats along with glee,
Waves tickle like poetry.
"What's next? A shipwrecked crab?
Or maybe a mermaid's jab?"

Upon each wave it wobbles,
Admiring seagulls and their troubles.
"Hey there, George! Don't be shy,
Join me for a crazy ride," it sighs.

In the end, it's just a log,
Maybe friends with a heavy fog.
But driftwood dreams don't make a splash,
Yet gather stories—and some trash.

Beneath the Surface of Time

Time's a fish that slips and spins,
With tales of losses, losses, wins.
It swishes past like a prankster,
Flipping flops with every stanza.

Looking down, what do I see?
A pair of socks from '93!
They're dancing, laughing, quite sublime,
Missing their match in ancient rhyme.

Here's a clock, just takes a dive,
In search for moments felt alive.
"Cannonball!" it makes a splash,
While memories swirl like a cash bash.

Time swims with bubbles and laughs,
Crafting memories like hand-drawn graphs.
So take a leap and don't be shy,
Join the circus as seconds fly!

Chasing the Horizon's Embrace

Running hard toward the sun,
With old flip-flops, I'm on the run.
A seagull squawks, "What's the fuss?"
I yell back, "Just chasing us!"

The horizon giggles in delight,
Waving back with skies so bright.
"Catch me if you can, my friend,
But you'll tire out before the end!"

Scrapes and bruises are the style,
With laughter riding each long mile.
"Wait for me!" I pant and yell,
While the sun starts to ring its bell.

Suddenly, it winks and slips,
Into the ocean with salty dips.
Horizon grins, with a knowing tease,
"Try again! I'm hard to please!"

The Flowing Canvas of Existence

Life's a canvas, what a mess,
Paint spills all, but no distress.
"Oops!" says blue with a hearty cheer,
As splashes add quirks, don't you hear?

Here's orange, looking quite surprised,
At how the world somehow connived.
"Let's blend!" cries red with a smile,
"Like jellybeans in a chocolate pile!"

Then green pops in, all lively and bold,
With purple on the side, now memory told.
Together they giggle, dance, and play,
In a world where colors have their say.

By the end of it, what a sight,
A wacky party, a true delight.
Life's a canvas, swirled and spun,
Embrace the chaos; we're not quite done!

Harvesting the Moonlight's Bounty

In dreams I see the moonlit glow,
With baskets big, I'm ready to go.
I harvest beams, all silver bright,
But trip on shadows in the night.

I tell the stars, 'You owe me cash!'
They wink and giggle, "Oh, what a splash!"
I count my loot, a cosmic gain,
Then spill it all—such bright disdain!

Tonight I'm rich, tomorrow's fun,
I'll trade moonlight for a cinnamon bun.
The baker laughs, says, "You're quite bold,
But moonlit riches are very cold!"

Yet here I stand with my lunar loot,
Who knew the moon could be so cute?
In the end, I guess it's quite clear,
I'll stick to treasures that reappear!

Gales that Shape the Soul

The winds, they howl, my hair a mess,
I blame the gales, they love this stress.
I set my sail to catch a breeze,
But end up tangled in the trees!

The birds just stare, as if to say,
"Is that a sailor or a cabaret?"
I juggle dreams with a gusty grin,
Who knew the wind could make me spin?

With every squall, I'm tossed about,
Like socks in laundry—left in doubt.
Yet laughter fills my flailing chase,
As I embrace this wild goose race!

So here's to gales that twist and shout,
I'll dance with storms and laugh it out.
For every storm that grips my soul,
Makes me the jester in life's roll!

Waves of Change

The ocean calls with a cheeky grin,
"Come ride the waves, let the fun begin!"
I hop on board, my balance a joke,
And wipe out hard—oh, what a poke!

The surfboards squeak, they mock my flair,
I crash like thunder, salt in my hair.
"Perfect timing!" the seagulls squawk,
As I bob along like a wobbly rock.

With every splash, I'm learning to flow,
Like spaghetti noodles in a bowl, you know?
Embracing tumbles, I'm free and wild,
Life's goofy seas, I'm still a child!

So here's to waves and change's tune,
With seaweed crowns and songs of the moon.
I'll ride this chaos until I'm blue,
For every wipeout, I find something new!

The Current Within

I dive right in, with splashes loud,
The current's swift, it draws a crowd.
I swim against, with all my might,
And find it's more like a water fight!

The fish give me a curious glance,
"Are you here for the swim or the dance?"
With flippers flapping, I swirl around,
Like an awkward crab that's lost its ground.

The river chuckles, "What a scene!"
I navigate like a clumsy machine.
With every twist, I laugh and grin,
The current's tug is a cheeky win!

So here's to swims that splash and splash,
Where giggles bubble up in a flash.
The current flows, and I'm along,
Dancing with fish to nature's song!

A Map of Stars Above

In the night, I lost my way,
Chasing stars, I took a sway.
The compass spun, then yelled, "Oh no!"
I ended up in a taco stand's glow!

With menus written in the sky,
I ordered nachos, oh my, oh my!
The stars just winked, they seemed to know,
That even in space, I'd find a show!

A comet zipped by with a wink attached,
"Don't worry, my friend, you've not quite hatched!"
I laughed and danced on the Milky Way,
Dreaming of snacks at the end of the play.

So here's to those who wander and roam,
In search of snacks, in search of home.
With laughter guiding every step we make,
We'll toast to fun with every mistake!

The Timekeeper's Ocean

In a sea of clocks, I took a dive,
Each tick and tock, it feels so alive.
But time went jelly, all wobbly and round,
And I surfed on seconds that couldn't be found!

A wave of minutes splashed on my face,
I giggled and floated, oh what a race!
The hourglass sharks swam with a grin,
Chasing the hours, so let the fun begin!

The sun set sideways, in a topsy-turvy way,
And time said, "Why not? Who's keeping the day?"
So I danced with seconds, just me and the tide,
Making memories that giggle and glide!

With laughter as my trusty sail,
I'll ride this ocean where moments prevail.
In the realm of moments, I'll always belong,
For the Timekeeper's ocean sings a silly song!

Serene Shores of Memory

At the beach of forget-me-nots blue,
I built sandcastles, who knew they'd skew?
A wave of laughter, a splash in the sun,
With all my memories, I'm never outdone!

Funny seashells whispered tales ever bright,
Of fish that wore hats, oh what a sight!
I traded seashells for giggles and grins,
With each silly story, the fun never thins!

Kites danced above with swirls of delight,
They tangled themselves in a marvelous flight.
On breezy adventures, I lost track of time,
For joy was the rhythm, and laughter, the rhyme!

So if you wander to those serene shores,
Remember the giggles that laughter restores.
In the sands of memory, we all leave our trace,
With smiles as seashells, an eternal embrace!

Embers Among the Waves

Beneath the stars where the fireflies play,
I sat on the beach, with night on display.
"Is that a critter?" I asked with a laugh,
As embers danced like they were taking a bath!

The waves told secrets that whispered so sweet,
With jokes and jests, they danced at my feet.
I threw in a marshmallow, oh what a blast,
The fire-spirits grinned, my treat was a blast!

Each ember chuckled, and I joined along,
A symphony of chuckles, an oceanic song.
With laughter as my lantern, I lit up the night,
And the waves joined the party, oh what a sight!

So come to the shore where the jokes never end,
With embers and waves, come let us blend.
In the glow of the night, we'll dance without cares,
For life's little moments are laughter's great flares!

Reflections in Saltwater Mirrors

If the waves could talk, they'd speak of fun,
And tell us tales of what they've done.
Flipping flops at the shore's grand show,
Sandcastles wobbly, oh what a woe!

Seagulls snatch fries with artful grace,
While children just run in a silly race.
The ocean's laughter bubbles and rolls,
Unpredictable as our lost socks' goals.

Sunburns resemble a lobster's plight,
While ice cream drips in the heat's delight.
Making sand angels, we fall and flop,
Waves wash our worries, a bubbly mop.

And when the sun sets with a wink and twirl,
We dance with the crabs, give it a whirl.
In saltwater mirrors, we find our way,
With giggles and splashes, we greet the day.

The Compass of the Heart

My heart's a compass, spins wild and free,
Pointing at pizza, or maybe ice tea.
It leads me in circles, a funny twist,
Like a lost sock in a laundry mist!

North feels like chips, or perhaps a nap,
South's just a couch and a cozy wrap.
East's all about morning coffee highs,
While West brings the laughter as the sun flies.

With friends as my compass, we make a map,
Through puddles and giggles, we happily lap.
Each wrong turn's a story, a tale to tell,
Like that time we got stuck in a jelly spell.

Navigating chaos with joy and glee,
A treasure hunt where the prize is just me!
My heart's a compass, always in play,
Finding the funny in every day.

Overcoming Storms of Emotion

Raindrops plop in a dance so absurd,
While feelings swirl, like a flock of birds.
Umbrellas flip inside out in a breeze,
And I just chuckle as I dodge the trees!

Dark clouds gather with an ominous frown,
Yet I find myself spinning and twirling around.
A laugh in the storm, with puddles to splash,
We navigate through, while the thunder will crash.

Crying's like rain, sometimes it pours,
But after that comes sunshine galore.
Sprinkling joy, like a rainbow's much sought,
Who knew emotions could be this hot?

We dance through the tempest, hating it not,
Winds toss our woes, yet we give it a shot.
For laughter's a sail, on this ship we grace,
Through storms and sunshine, we find our place.

Embracing the Unknown

With curious eyes, I peek around,
At all the things yet to be found.
In life's big closet, I search for fun,
With treasures hidden, but where's my bun?

Jumping into puddles, oh what a splash,
Each moment's a game, it happens so fast.
What lies ahead? A cake or a mess?
Maybe a wild goose chase for some stress!

The fear of the "what ifs" makes me grin,
Like a cat with yarn, I'll take it on the chin.
Life's a buffet of wobbly treats,
With surprises that dance on wobbly feet.

So here's to the paths we haven't explored,
With giggles and snacks, we can't be ignored.
Embracing the unknown, we paint the sky,
With laughter and love, we're sure to fly.

The Lighthouses of Wisdom

In the foggy mist we sail,
Chasing wisdom's silly trail.
A lighthouse winks, with chuckles bright,
Guiding us through the comical night.

With every wave, a story spins,
Of quirky braves and their silly sins.
A seagull laughs, oh what a sight,
As we trip on the docks in the pale moonlight.

The stars above, like wisecracks twinkle,
While we dance like fools, our laughter's sprinkle.
Forgotten maps and hats askew,
Ahoy, mateys! Here's a laugh or two!

So raise a toast to silly strife,
For every fall, there's joy in life.
With lighthouses guiding our jovial quest,
We'll steer through giggles and find our best!

Cascading Reflections

In puddles deep, reflections play,
Jumping in like kids—hip hip hooray!
They say it's wise to think it through,
But splashing's fun, who needs a clue?

With every drop, a chuckle spills,
As life's a prankster, giving thrills.
We catch our smiles in raindrops clear,
And dance around without a fear.

The mirror's game is quite absurd,
Why look for sense when laughs are stirred?
In laughter's grip, we'll learn to rise,
Reflecting joy—what a surprise!

So here's to splashes, laughter, and play,
Cascading giggles brighten the way.
Let's float downstream, together we glide,
In puddles of joy, side by side!

Solstice of the Soul

When the sun's high, we wear our shades,
While time drips slow, laughter parades.
A dance-off's brewing, with tunes so bold,
Even shadows join with stories told.

The longest day, with goofy tricks,
As sunburned noses pull funny flicks.
We chase the light, in flip-flops fly,
Who knew my dance moves could touch the sky?

While the moon waits, with a wink, it plays,
As we get lost in endless haze.
A party's brewing, come one, come all,
In the solstice glow, let's laugh and sprawl!

With spirits high, and hearts so bright,
We revel in joy, from day to night.
So here's to warmth, and fun, and cheer,
Join the solstice dance—let's disappear!

The Horizon's Embrace

Beyond the waves, a view so grand,
Where dreams are mixed with grains of sand.
We wave at clouds, they wave right back,
Setting sail on our laughter track.

The sun dips low, a clown in the sky,
As we race the seagulls, oh how they fly!
Each sunset whispers a quirky tale,
With colors that giggle, and boats that sail.

In the embrace of the horizon's glow,
Life's funny antics steal the show.
We'll dance with shadows, till stars ignite,
With every step, find joy, take flight!

So here's to laughter, so bright, so wide,
Embracing horizons, like the ocean tide.
With friends beside us, what a carefree chase,
In the funny dance, we find our place!

Chasing the Horizon

I chased the sun, it ran so fast,
My legs grew tired, I fell at last.
The seagulls laughed, they knew my plight,
I waved at clouds, oh what a sight!

A surfboard's dream, a sailboat's tease,
I tried to surf on a gentle breeze.
But every wave just flipped me back,
I ended up in a sandwich sack!

I thought I'd fly, I brought a kite,
But it tangled me in sheer delight.
I soared and dipped, a roller dance,
And ended up with ants in my pants!

Now here I am, on shores of jest,
Chasing horizons, I'll take a rest.
I'll sip some seaweed, with a grin so wide,
And imagine my boat—left high and dry!

Winds of Transformation

A gust swept through my hat away,
It did a dance, it went astray.
I ran behind, like a clumsy fool,
Waving my arms, oh, what a rule!

The breeze said, "Come, let's have some fun!"
It tickled my nose just like a pun.
I laughed so hard, I lost my grip,
On the sandwich I brought for my trip!

A balloon floated, bright and bold,
I grabbed a string, oh, what a hold.
But up it went, to the skies so blue,
I sighed and thought, I'm stuck here too!

Yet in this whirl, I found my cheer,
The winds transformed my age-old fear.
So I'll let go, and dance along,
With every gust, I sing my song!

Echoes from the Abyss

I dropped my phone, it sunk so deep,
I heard it ring from the ocean's keep.
"Hello!" it chimed, in a whale's own way,
I laughed so loud, then what a play!

A sardine laughed, with fins so sleek,
"Join us!" it bubbled, "that's the peak!"
I kicked and splashed, oh what a scene,
A dance party hosted by fish and sea queen!

But then a crab pinched my toe just right,
Gave me a hop, oh what a fright!
I scrambled up, with a fishy frown,
While seaweed giggled, "Let's go down!"

As echoes formed in underwater glee,
I waved goodbye to my phone, carefree.
The waves they danced, in laughter's bliss,
And I joined in, not a thing amiss!

Compass of Hope

I found a compass, it spun around,
Pointing to places, yet none I found.
It sent me left, then right, then round,
While I just stood, quite lost and browned.

"Where to, friend?" I asked in jest,
It blinked a light, as though it'd guessed.
"Follow your heart, just don't let it sink,
Or you might end up with a shoe full of ink!"

With each misstep, I danced on sand,
Creating footprints, unplanned and grand.
The compass laughed, it wobbled bold,
"Just wander free, let stories unfold!"

So here I am, with joy in tow,
A merry wanderer, the compass in tow.
In this silly game, I dance and cope,
For every step leads to more than hope!

Whalesong of the Soul

In the ocean deep, a whale takes a dive,
Singing to dolphins, making them thrive.
With bubbles and laughs, they dance by the shore,
Chasing each other till they fall to the floor.

A crab wears a hat, what a curious sight,
While seaweed sways, caught in the light.
The jellyfish giggles whilst drifting along,
Making up lyrics to a silly song.

Starfish high-fives as they slide on the sand,
A parade of silliness, all perfectly planned.
With fish wearing shades and a clam doing flips,
Life in the ocean is full of good quips.

So join in the fun, let your worries go,
As we ride on the waves, putting on a show.
In this underwater world, laughter takes flight,
Singing whales echo our joy, oh what delight!

In Search of the Lighthouse

A sailor named Lou took a stroll in the fog,
With maps made of toast, and a cat named Bog.
He squinted and shouted, "Where's that bright beam?"
But the lighthouse just chuckled, or so it would seem.

Seagulls on scooters zoomed past in a whirl,
While mermaids flipped coins and made wishes that swirled.
Lou tripped on a pirate; they both shared a laugh,
As the fish lent a fin, taking turns with a gaff.

A crab with a compass, lost in its route,
Joined Lou on his quest, in search of the scout.
Their shenanigans caused quite the ruckus and cheer,
As they stumbled on treasures, and souvenirs dear.

Finally they laughed, "The lighthouse is here!"
But it turned out to be just a big pint of beer.
So they clinked their mugs, and the tales came alive,
As Lou found the light, in a relishable dive!

Horizon Dancers

Underneath the sun, the crabs put on shoes,
With jazz in the air, they danced to their blues.
A tortoise wore shades, giving pointers to all,
While a clam's doing cha-cha, not caring at all.

Seashells are spinning, what a quirky ballet,
While the fish orchestrate, in a splashy array.
A dolphin in tux, leads the fancy parade,
As the ocean's a stage, where no dreams are delayed.

The horizon shines bright, drawing laughs from afar,
As seagulls deliver giggles in a jar.
They glide and they swoop, what a hilarious sight,
While waves keep the rhythm all through the night.

So let's join the dance, and swirl with delight,
Chasing sunbeams above, in the warm moonlight.
With joy in the currents, we'll shimmy and sway,
While laughing and spinning, we'll sail through the day!

Crosswinds of Change

A kite caught a breeze, soaring high in the air,
While a dog tried to chase it, with a curious stare.
The cat rolled her eyes, unimpressed by the fuss,
As wind sang a tune, making laughter combust.

Old shoes in the alley, their stories retold,
Whispering secrets of adventures so bold.
While squirrels on skateboards zoom past in a flash,
Governed by laughter, like a rambunctious bash.

A wheelbarrow races, feeling quite spry,
With flowers in tow, waving 'bye' to the sky.
As trees sway and bend, sharing gossip so grand,
With whispers of change, painting life's hand.

So embrace silly moments, when breezes draw near,
For change brings the giggles, amidst every cheer.
With laughter our compass, we happily roam,
Through winds that will carry us safely back home!

The Journeying Star

Oh, the star that rolled away,
From its comfy sky-blue bed,
Dancing down the Milky Way,
Laughing, 'Leave the world to Fred!'

With a wink, it took a dive,
Into the ocean's bubbly tales,
"Here, I can truly thrive,
Better than those boring snails!"

It surfed on waves of giggles,
Told the fishy jokes they know,
As seagulls pulled the wiggles,
Oh, what fun, that star in tow!

"Keep your shoes and keep your socks,
I'll wear a cloud, it suits me best!
I'll dodge the waves and silly rocks,
Life's a silly, flying jest!"

Secrets of the Salty Breeze

The salty breeze has secrets,
It tickles toes and whispers tales,
Of jellyfish in polka-dot nets,
And crabby dance-off fails!

It carries scents of fishy fries,
And tales of sandcastles gone rogue,
Whimsical winds and cheeky sighs,
Scoffing at the weighty frog!

"Why be serious?" it asks with glee,
"Flip-flops are the fanciest shoes!
Join me in a salty spree,
Dodge the seagull's fearsome snooze!"

With a whoosh and twirl, it swept the beach,
Promising laughter as it sped,
Underneath its breezy speech,
A sea of snickers; I was led!

A Map of Memories

Here's a map made out of dreams,
With Xs that mark laughter's shores,
Directions filled with silly schemes,
Cross paths with clumsily closed doors.

A route for fumbles, slips, and falls,
Where giggly moments get their say,
Wobbly stunts and laughing calls,
Follow the zigzags of the spray!

Find the treasure of the time,
Where ice cream drips melt into fun,
Discover jokes that softly rhyme,
And dance until the day is done!

So grab a map—don't look so blue!
Let's wander where the laughter glows,
Forget the stern and usual view,
And chase the breeze as it blows!

Beyond the Breakers

What lies beyond those crashing waves?
A land where silly giggles reign,
Where clumsy fish and eagle braves,
Trade silly tales for friendly gain.

A place where jelly jumps and hops,
And seaweed dances on its own,
Where every splash, the laughter pops,
And no one feels completely grown!

With octopuses dressed in style,
And clowns of coral, bright and bold,
We'll laugh and swim a merry mile,
Away from worries, into gold!

So come on, friend, let's take the plunge,
Leave behind the serious shores,
To where the splashes laugh and lunge,
Beyond the breakers, fun restores!

Currents of Growth

In life's great sea, I found a shoe,
The left from the right—who knew?
I walked a mile, then took a break,
To rescue a fish, from a big mistake.

The waves rolled in with a playful splash,
A seagull swooped down for a quick snack.
I said, 'Hey buddy, that's not for you!'
But he just laughed, and off he flew.

I plant my seeds in sand, not soil,
In hopes they sprout and give me joy.
But the only thing that seems to thrive,
Are the quirky weeds that come alive!

So here I stand, a dandy fool,
With jokes and laughs, my favorite tool.
For growth is more than silent cheer,
It's giggles and grins that keep life near!

The Ocean of Experience

I dove into life with a belly flop,
Making waves that made the seagulls stop.
With each failed attempt, I learned to glide,
Though most times I found I'd crash, then slide.

Oh! How I quested for treasure and pearls,
Only to find tangled seaweed swirls.
My map was smudged, my compass askew,
Ahoy! Those directions led me to stew!

For every storm that shook my boat,
I'd just crack jokes and keep it afloat.
With laughter as my sail, I twist and twirl,
Navigating life—what a silly whirl!

So here's to the ocean's messy delight,
Where waves tickle toes and stars shine bright.
In each splash and laugh, I've found a friend,
The journey is funny—on that, depend!

Sailor's Soliloquy

On my little boat, I sang out loud,
'The wind is my friend, I'm feeling proud!'
But a gust of breeze tossed me about,
I tripped on a fish, and then I pout!

With jellyfish hats and a starfish crew,
We swayed and danced, what a silly view!
I asked the waves to teach me their ways,
But they just rolled back, in playful sways.

I tried to fish with a rubber band,
Caught a sock instead, wasn't that grand?
The octopus laughed, waving goodbye,
I waved back with a wink in my eye.

So with each leap that I made from the dock,
I found that life's a humorous frock.
With giggles and gaffes, I sail with glee,
A funny sailor's life—just suited for me!

Beyond the Dunes

I wandered past the dunes so high,
Thought I'd find a treasure, oh my!
But what I found were socks and shoes,
A beachcomber's delight, nothing to lose!

Seagulls squawked in their silly dance,
While I attempted a wobbly prance.
I tumbled down, covered in sand,
The dunes laughed loudly—I'm in demand!

I built a castle, won't it be grand?
Till it washed away, my dreams unmanned.
Yet, with a smile, I grab my pail,
And start again—oh, what a tale!

So here I stand, the sun at my back,
With laughter echoing—no need to track.
The journey's a giggle, a fun little run,
In the land of dunes, where all is fun!

Odyssey of the Unseen

In a boat that's barely afloat,
I navigate with a soggy coat.
The map's upside down, can't find my way,
Must have been reading it on laundry day.

Seagulls squawk with a judgmental glare,
While I fumble with snacks, flying everywhere.
A fish jumped in, took my sandwich too,
Guess even he knows, life's a hullabaloo!

Waves slap my side like an old friend's joke,
I laugh out loud, though I'm feeling broke.
With a splash and a splash, I drift around,
Who knew survival could be this profound?

So here's to the trip, with all its blunders,
As I ponder the universe, dodging thunders.
Though I'm soaked and lost in my quest,
At least I'm the captain of this messy fest!

The Rhythm of the Waves

Waves dance like nobody's watching,
But trust me, I'm here, totally botching.
I tried to surf, ended up in the sand,
Turns out balance isn't quite my brand.

Children shriek as their kites try to fly,
While my umbrella prefers to say goodbye.
I wave at the fish, who seem to object,
While I'm just hoping my swimsuit won't defect.

A dolphin jumped by, gave a wink and a nod,
As I flailed about, feeling rather odd.
Life's just a splash of clumsy delight,
With giggles and splashes, oh what a sight!

So here I am, just swaying away,
In the rhythm of splashes, come what may.
Laughing at myself, in this watery swirl,
Being the captain of my own frank world.

Bridges Over Troubled Waters

I built a bridge with my morning toast,
But it crumbled fast, which I love the most.
With coffee in hand and a pancake hat,
I greet the day like a worn-out brat.

Oh, look at that! A bridge over fries,
Where seagulls plot and the ketchup lies.
They circle above like they're in a play,
While I dodge their droppings, come what may.

Traffic's a mess on this culinary stream,
With jellyfish jelly and a marshmallow dream.
So here I stand, a major flop,
Building bridges while my snack breaks crop!

But laughter's the glue in turbulent times,
While I trip and fall, making silly rhymes.
So join me now, on this food-laden spree,
Where bridges are tasty and life's just a spree!

Secrets Beneath the Surface

I dipped my toes, and oh, what a find,
A sea cucumber that seemed quite blind.
He wiggled around, gave me quite a start,
I guess his charm was just off the chart.

Coral reefs sing in colors so bright,
While I'm here searching for lost flip-flops in fright.
A crab then pinched my toe just for fun,
Turns out he wanted to share a pun!

Dolphins whisper secrets, oh, can't you see?
They're gossiping wildly, about you and me!
I wave them off with a splash and a grin,
These underwater tales just tickle my skin.

So dive with me deep, where giggles abide,
In the currents of chaos, with silliness wide.
For life's just a party beneath the blue,
Where laughter's the treasure that's waiting for you!

Shores of Discovery

On the beach, I found a shoe,
It was one, just one, who knew?
A crab danced by, with a wink and grin,
I asked him if he'd like to fin.

Seagulls squawked, stealing my fries,
I swore they plotted in disguise.
With laughter loud, they swooped and dove,
While I just wanted to tan and loaf.

A toddler built a sand-strong wall,
And then fell in—it was quite the fall!
We cheered him on, his dreams galore,
As the ocean whispered, "Build some more!"

So here I sit, with sand in my shoes,
But hey, what else could a poet choose?
With laughter and fun, my heart sets sail,
On shores of discovery, I shall prevail!

Riptides of Emotion

A wave crashed in and stole my hat,
I chased it down, how 'bout that?
It spun and twirled like a circus act,
   Too bad it was a seaweed pact.

My friend cried out, "Don't lose your head!"
But my hat was off, it was well-read.
He glided past in a rubber duck,
I tossed him snacks—my luck was stuck!

Jumping in, we surfed the bubble,
Squealed like kids—oh, what a trouble!
The ocean roared, "You think you're slick?"
But we just laughed, let us do the trick.

Emotions ebbed like the moonlit tide,
With chuckles and splashes, we'd never hide.
In the whirlpool of joy, we take our chances,
Riptides of emotion lead to wild dances!

Distant Horizons

A ship sailed far, with snacks on board,
The captain grinned; it was quite the hoard!
Off we went, with sails so white,
To distant horizons, oh what a sight!

The sky was blue, the waves did play,
A dolphin leaped—hip hip hooray!
A seagull squawked, "You're lost, my friend,"
But we just shrugged, this fun won't end.

We spotted whales; they waved their tails,
As laughter echoed through our gales.
With every wave, we cheered 'huzzah!',
For distant horizons, our hearts would draw.

Each sunset brought a dance so bright,
With twirls and giggles fading light.
We'll sail these seas, with joy to find,
For distant horizons, we are aligned!

The Driftwood Chronicles

Found driftwood shaped like a monkey,
I called it George; it was quite funky!
We built a fort, a kingdom grand,
With seashell treasures all at hand.

A starfish joined the royal court,
Declaring fish as the main sport.
We laughed and played, till dusk set in,
With wild tales of how we'd win.

Seagulls acted as our royal spies,
Reporting on the level of fries.
The tide came in, a morn surprise,
And swept away our royal guise.

Yet through it all, with smiles so wide,
We embraced the waves, the ebbing tide.
In the chronicles of driftwood grand,
We found our joy in the sand.

Whispers of the Wandering Waves

The ocean's voice is quite a tease,
It tickles toes, just like a breeze.
With every splash, I jump and yelp,
A dancing fish says, "Join me, kelp!"

Seashells giggle beneath my feet,
They dress in sand – oh, what a treat!
The seagulls squawk, a honking choir,
Each wave a joke, and I retire!

Flip-flops flying, in the air,
My beach hat's lost without a care.
The Sun's a prankster, burning bright,
I apply sunblock, but miss a sight!

So here I stand, like a big ol' clown,
In my swimsuit that's two sizes down.
With laughter echoing through the surf,
Life's frothy fun, beyond the turf.

Echoes of an Endless Shore

The shore is full of whispers loud,
Where crabs perform, and crowds are proud.
Each wave rolls in to steal my hat,
While seagulls laugh, 'Hey, how about that?'

My picnic basket takes a trip,
A raccoon joins, gives me the slip.
Sandwiches fly, it's quite the feast,
Nature's pests turn into a beast!

The sun reflects one winky eye,
As I dodge jellyfish, oh my!
Each splash invites a silly fate,
As laughter bounces, can't quite wait!

In this circus of ocean cheer,
I find my heart, a little deer.
With every echo, giggles soar,
The beach is where I'm evermore!

Currents of Hope and Despair

Floating dreams on rubber ducks,
Lost my sunscreen - oh, what luck!
The waves surf in on a secret scheme,
While I paddle hard, but can't quite beam!

A crab named Larry steals my fries,
He boasts of dance moves and funny ties.
Splashing here, there, to steal a peek,
I laugh so hard, it's now a leak!

Life's a surfboard on a wild ride,
With giggles and splashes, I can't hide.
Diving deep into a barrage of foam,
Yet every tumble feels like home.

A wave bows low, just like a friend,
Saying, "No worries, it's just pretend!"
And as I wipe the sea from my face,
I find joy in this chaotic place.

The Dance of Distant Horizons

Out where the sky meets blushing seas,
I twirl and dip with ocean breeze.
Shells on the shore are my ballet shoes,
While dolphins giggle, "You can't lose!"

With a flip and a flop, I launch a shrimp,
It somersaults, does a joyful sprint.
Pretend to surf on a tidal wave,
Yet here I am, a wobbly slave!

The lighthouse blinks with a wink or two,
It knows my moves, and it laughs too.
Fish start a conga, the sun claps loud,
In my dance-off, I'm blissfully proud!

So let the horizon shift and twirl,
In every splash, I seek a whirl.
With laughter ringing, I float and glide,
In my goofy waltz, I'll take the ride.

Castaways on the Isle of Reflection

We've washed ashore with funny hair,
Searching for snacks, but it's just thin air.
Our boats went adrift, what a silly plight,
Now we barter seashells for a bite at night.

The crabs are our council, they rule with claws,
Holding deep meetings with nary a pause.
We laugh as we ponder our choices so wild,
But who's keeping score? We're all just beguiled.

The sun is our clock, it spins round and round,
While fish throw a party, our cheers abound.
We're kings of the beach with no royal decree,
Just don't ask us how to get back to the sea.

Tomorrow we'll sail on coconuts' backs,
With pirate maps made from old snack pack stacks.
We'll dance in the surf and take life in stride,
Castaways forever, with laughs as our guide.

Driftings of Destiny

We set out in boats made of hopes and of dreams,
But drifted down rivers that flow with ice creams.
Our paddles are spoons, we're stirring the fun,
With laughter as fuel, we'll ride till we're done.

The fish are our crew, they flash toothy grins,
While seagulls above claim victory wins.
Our compass is broken, it points to the fries,
No map to follow, just clear summer skies.

Each wave is a chance to trip on our toes,
We dance with the currents and no one just knows.
Drifting along on this ridiculous sea,
Where life's just a joke, and we're laughing with glee.

When night falls like velvet and stars start to blink,
We toast to the mischief with soda to drink.
Our journey uncharted, our spirits so light,
In driftings of destiny, we're just here for the bite.

A Symphony of Changing Currents

A symphony plays in the waves and the foam,
With seaweed as violins and crabs as our home.
The gulls are the choirs, they squawk out of tune,
While we tap our feet to the song of the moon.

Each splash is a note, each ripple a sound,
As fish join the chorus, they jump all around.
We'll waltz with the dolphins, tango with rays,
In this crazy concert, we'll dance for days.

The ocean may giggle and bubble with cheer,
As we take all our chances, our worries unclear.
Laughing at memories that drift like the breeze,
With joy in abundance and salty hair we seize.

So raise up your cups filled with sea salt and glee,
For life's just a riddle, a fun jamboree.
A symphony of currents, forever we'll sway,
In this humorous ocean where we love to play.

The Call of Distant Echoes

Hear the echoes calling from far and near,
Stories of whimsy and laughter we hear.
The rocks all gossip, they talk of old tales,
As we skip on the shore with our wobbly gales.

The sand shouts out riddles, we scratch our heads,
Unraveling mysteries in our sandy beds.
A clam plays the spoons while starfish tap dance,
We join in the fun, giving chaos a chance.

Whispers of walruses tickle our ears,
Toasting to journeys and funny career fears.
The ocean's our playground, no need for a plan,
Just follow the echoes, wherever they can.

With each wave that crashes, we giggle and glide,
Life's full of quirks, take it all in stride.
The call of the echoes, a beacon so bright,
Guides us through laughter, from morning to night.

www.ingramcontent.com/pod-product-compliance
Lightning Source LLC
Chambersburg PA
CBHW050307120526
44590CB00016B/2532